Book Title: Paolo Maldini Italian Football Legend

Chapter Titles:
1. A Football Fa
2. The Making of a Legend: Youth Career
3. The Rise of AC Milan: Professional Debut
4. The Golden Age: AC Milan's Era of Dominance
5. The Italian Stallions: Success with the National Team
6. The Captain: Leadership on and off the Field
7. The Art of Defending: Defensive Techniques
8. The Lasting Partnership: Maldini and Nesta's Defensive Dominance
9. The End of an Era: Retirement
10. The Milan Director: Role in Club Management
11. The Family Man: Personal Life
12. The Fashion Icon: Influence on Style
13. The Philanthropist: Charitable Work
14. The Global Icon: Impact on Football Worldwide
15. The Legacy Continues: Influence on Future Generations

0.
INTRODUCTION:

Paolo Maldini is one of the most celebrated footballers in the history of the sport. As the son of Cesare Maldini, who was also a football legend, Paolo was destined for greatness from a young age. His incredible skill, dedication, and leadership abilities propelled him to the top of the football world, where he achieved numerous victories, awards, and accolades.

Throughout his career, Maldini was known for his technical skill, agility, and exceptional defensive abilities. He was a key member of the famous AC Milan team that dominated football in the 1990s and early 2000s. He also achieved great success with the Italian national team, helping them to win the 1988 UEFA European Championship and reach the final of the 1994 FIFA World Cup.

In addition to his outstanding career on the pitch,

Maldini has also made significant contributions to the world of football off the pitch. He has been involved in club management and has also worked to promote the sport globally. In this book, we will explore Maldini's life and legacy, delving into his early years, his success with AC Milan and the national team, his personal life, and his post-playing career.

1. A FOOTBALL FAMILY - THE MALDINI LEGACY

As the son of a legendary footballer, Paolo Maldini had some big shoes to fill. But he was determined to make his mark on the sport that had been such a big part of his family's life for generations.

Paolo's father, Cesare Maldini, had been a star defender for AC Milan and the Italian national team. His grandfather, Aldo Maldini, had also played for Milan in the 1930s. Football was in Paolo's blood, and he started playing as soon as he could walk.

Growing up in Milan, Paolo spent countless hours kicking a ball around with his brother and sister in the backyard. Their father was a demanding coach, but he also knew how to have fun with the kids. He would take them to matches and training, teaching them the ins and outs of the game from a young age.

By the time Paolo was a teenager, he was already being scouted by some of Italy's top clubs. But he knew he wanted to follow in his father's footsteps and play for Milan. He joined the youth academy and worked his way up through the ranks.

Paolo made his debut for Milan in 1985, at the age of 16. He quickly established himself as a talented and reliable defender, with a knack for reading the game and making crucial tackles. He played for Milan for his entire career, spanning three decades, and became one of the greatest players in the club's history.

Paolo's sons, Daniel and Christian, also inherited the family's footballing genes. They both played for Milan's youth teams and went on to have successful careers in the sport. Daniel even followed in his father's footsteps and became a defender for Milan and the Italian national team.

The Maldini family's legacy in football is a testament to the power of passion, dedication, and hard work. They are a shining example of how a love for the game can run deep in a family's veins, and how that love can inspire greatness on the pitch.

As Paolo reflects on his family's legacy, he feels grateful for the opportunities that football has given him and his loved ones. He knows that the game has the power to bring people together, create unforgettable memories, and inspire the next generation of players.

In the end, the Maldini legacy is not just about the trophies and accolades. It's about the joy of the game, the thrill of competition, and the bond that is formed between teammates, coaches, and fans. It's a legacy that will endure for generations to come.

Paolo Maldini couldn't be prouder of his family's legacy in football. For him, it's not just about the success they achieved on the pitch, but also about the lessons they learned from it.

Football taught Paolo and his family the value of teamwork, discipline, and perseverance. They learned how to work together towards a common goal, how to push themselves to their limits, and how to bounce back from defeat.

But football also gave them a sense of community and belonging. The Maldives have always been deeply connected to Milan, both the city and the football club. They have seen how the game can bring people together, create shared experiences, and foster a sense of pride and identity.

For Paolo, being a part of Milan was always more than just a job. It was a way of life. He felt a deep sense of responsibility to represent the club and the city with the utmost professionalism and dedication. He knew that every time he stepped onto the pitch, he was not just playing for himself, but for the thousands of fans who supported him and the team.

Now that he's retired, Paolo is passing on his love for the game to the next generation. He's involved in youth coaching and mentoring, and he's always looking for ways to give back to the sport that has given him so much.

But even as he looks to the future, Paolo will always cherish the memories of his playing days. The roar of the crowd, the thrill of victory, the bonds forged with his teammates – these are moments that will stay with him forever.

In the end, the Maldini legacy is not just a story of footballing success. It's a story of passion, commitment, and love – for the game, for the club, and for each other. It's a story that continues to inspire, amuse, and educate football fans around the world.

2. THE MAKING OF A LEGEND: YOUTH CAREER

Paolo Maldini's journey to footballing greatness began at a young age. Growing up in Milan, he was surrounded by the sport from the moment he was born. His father, Cesare Maldini, was a star defender for AC Milan and the Italian national team, and he instilled a love for the game in his son from the very beginning.

Paolo's talent was evident from a young age. He had a natural ability to read the game, make crucial tackles, and create chances for his teammates. His father recognized this early on and began coaching him in the backyard, teaching him the fundamentals of the sport and encouraging him to play with passion and intensity.

Paolo's youth career was defined by his time in

Milan's youth academy. He joined the club at the age of 10 and quickly rose through the ranks, impressing coaches and teammates with his skill and dedication.

As a youth player, Paolo was known for his versatility. He could play as a central defender, a full-back, or a defensive midfielder, and he excelled in each position. He had a keen tactical mind and an ability to read the game that was well beyond his years.

In 1984, at the age of 16, Paolo was called up to train with the senior team for the first time. He was nervous and excited, but he quickly proved that he belonged. The senior players were impressed with his composure, his technique, and his work rate, and they welcomed him into the squad with open arms.

Paolo's debut for Milan came the following year, in a match against Udinese. He was just 16 years old at the time, but he played with the confidence and maturity of a seasoned professional. He made several crucial tackles and helped his team to a 1-0 victory.

From that moment on, Paolo was a regular in Milan's senior team. He played in almost every match, and he quickly became one of the team's most important players. He won his first Serie A title with Milan in 1988, and he went on to win many more over the course of his career.

Paolo's youth career was the foundation for his

success as a professional. It was where he honed his skills, developed his tactical knowledge, and learned the value of hard work and discipline. It was also where he forged lifelong bonds with his teammates, coaches, and fans – bonds that would stay with him throughout his career and beyond.

For Paolo, his youth career was not just a stepping stone to greatness – it was an essential part of his journey, a time of learning, growth, and discovery. It was where he began to realize the full extent of his potential, and where he began to dream of the glory that lay ahead.

As he progressed through the youth ranks, Paolo's talent and potential became more and more evident. His father Cesare, who had become a coach by this point, continued to mentor and guide him, helping him to refine his technique and develop his game.

But Paolo's success was not just down to natural ability and good coaching. He also possessed a fierce determination and a work ethic that set him apart from his peers. He was always one of the first to arrive at training and one of the last to leave, putting in extra hours on the pitch and in the gym to improve his strength, speed, and agility.

This dedication and focus paid off in spades. By the time he made his debut for Milan, he was already a well-rounded player with a deep understanding of the game. He was able to read the play, anticipate the movements of his opponents, and make crucial interventions when needed.

But what set Paolo apart was his composure under pressure. Even at a young age, he was able to stay calm and focused in the face of adversity, whether it was a hostile crowd, a tough opponent, or a high-stakes match. He had a natural leadership ability that inspired his teammates and earned him the respect of his rivals.

Paolo's youth career was not without its challenges. He suffered his fair share of setbacks and disappointments, and he had to work hard to overcome them. But he never lost his love for the game or his belief in his bails.

Looking back on those early years, Paolo is grateful for the support and guidance he received from his family, his coaches, and his teammates. He knows that without them, he would not have achieved the success he did.

Today, as a coach and mentor himself, Paolo is determined to pass on the lessons he learned as a young player to the next generation of footballers. He knows that talent alone is not enough to make it in the world of professional football – it takes hard work, discipline, and a willingness to learn and grow.

For Paolo, the lessons of his youth career – the importance of dedication, focus, and resilience – are just as relevant today as they were when he was a young player. And they are a vital part of the Maldini legacy, a legacy that continues to inspire and motivate footballers around the world.

3. THE RISE OF AC MILAN: PROFESSIONAL DEBUT

Paolo Maldini's professional debut for AC Milan was a landmark moment in the history of the club. It was the beginning of a new era of success, built on the foundations of hard work, talent, and a deep understanding of the game.

At just 16 years old, Paolo was already a highly regarded prospect. But few could have predicted just how quickly he would establish himself as one of the finest defenders in the world.

His debut came in a Serie A match against Udinese, and from the first whistle, it was clear that he belonged on the pitch. He was calm and composed, making crucial tackles and interceptions and playing with a maturity that belied his age.

As the season progressed, Paolo's performances continued to impress. He formed a formidable partnership with Franco Baresi, the veteran defender who had already established himself as one of Milan's all-time greats. Together, they marshallmarshaledkline with skill and precision, shutting down opposing attacks and providing a platform for Milan's forwards to do their work.

Milan went on to win the Serie A title that season, and Paolo played a crucial role in the team's success. He was named the league's best young player, an accolade that confirmed what many already knew – that he was a star in the making.

Over the years that followed, Paolo continued to go from strength to strength. He became a regular fixture in the Milan team, earning the captain's armband at just 22 years old. He played in eight Champions League finals, winning five, and he helped Milan to secure numerous domestic titles.

But despite all his success, Paolo remained humble and grounded. He knew that football was a team sport, and he was quick to credit his teammates, coaches, and fans for their role in his achievements. He also continued to work hard, constantly striving to improve his game and stay at the top of his profession.

Today, Paolo's legacy at Milan is secure. He is

widely regarded as one of the greatest defenders in the history of the game, and his name is synonymous with the club he served so faithfully for over two decades. His professionalism, skill, and leadership continue to inspire footballers around the world, and his contribution to the game will be remembered for generations to come.

Throughout his career, Paolo Maldini played an integral role in the rise of AC Milan as a European football powerhouse. His leadership and defensive prowess helped to shape the club's success and cement its status as one of the greatest teams in football history.

During his time at Milan, Paolo formed strong bonds with his teammates and coaches, becoming an important figure both on and off the pitch. He was respected for his intelligence, work ethic, and tactical acumen, and his influence was felt throughout the team.

But it was his performances on the pitch that truly set him apart. He was a master of his craft, combining outstanding positional sense, impeccable timing, and a fierce competitive spirit to become one of the most feared defenders of his generation.

Opponents knew that they would have to be at their best to get past Paolo, and even then, they might not succeed. He was a natural leader and a born winner, and he pushed his teammates to be their best every time they stepped onto the pitch.

Paolo's ability to read the game was second to none. He had an instinctive understanding of the flow of a match, knowing when to press forward and when to sit back and defend. His composure under pressure was remarkable, and he always seemed to make the right decisions at the right time.

As the years went by, Paolo's reputation continued to grow. He became a true icon of Italian football, and his name was synonymous with Milan's success. He remained an integral part of the team until his retirement at the age of 41, leaving behind a legacy that few will ever match.

Today, Paolo's impact on Milan and football as a whole is still being felt. His passion for the game and his commitment to excellence continue to inspire footballers around the world, and his place in the pantheon of football greats is assured. He is a true legend of the sport, and his legacy will endure for generations to come.

4. THE GOLDEN AGE: AC ERA OF DOMINANCE

The Golden Age of Paolo Maldini was a period of unparalleled success for AC Milan. With Paolo as their leader and talisman, the team dominated Italian and European football for much of the 1990s and early 2000s, winning numerous titles and establishing themselves as one of the greatest teams in football history.

At the heart of Milan's success was their rock-solid defense, led by Paolo and his long-time partner Franco Baresi. Together, they formed one of the most formidable defensive partnerships in the game, using their intelligence, skill, and experience to shut down opposing attacks and keep clean sheets.

But it wasn't just in defense that Paolo shone. He

was also an accomplished attacking player, capable of contributing to his team's goals with his accurate passing, clever movement, and lethal left foot. He was a complete player, able to influence the game in all areas of the pitch.

During the Golden Age of Paolo Maldini, Milan won an astonishing array of titles. They lifted the Serie A trophy seven times, the Italian Cup five times, and the Supercoppa Italiana four times. They also won the UEFA Champions League five times, including two in a row in 1989 and 1990.

Paolo was a key player in all of these triumphs, and his influence on the team cannot be overstated. He led by example, setting the standard for his teammates with his work rate, professionalism, and dedication to the team's success.

Off the pitch, Paolo was also a model professional. He was known for his impeccable conduct and his respect for the game, and he was a role model for young players everywhere. He embodied the values of AC Milan, and he helped to create a culture of excellence and respect that endures to this day.

In many ways, the Golden Age of Paolo Maldini represented the pinnacle of Milan's success. It was a time of dominance and achievement, driven by the talent, intelligence, and leadership of one of football's all-time greats. For Milan fans, it was a period to be savored and remembered for generations to come.

One of the most iconic moments of the Golden Age of Paolo Maldini was undoubtedly the 2003 UEFA Champions League final, held at Old Trafford in Manchester. Milan faced off against Italian rivals Juventus in what would prove to be a dramatic and hard-fought match.

Paolo was at his very best on that night, leading Milan's defense with age and determination. He made a number several interceptions and tackles, and his reading of the game was flawless. Juventus struggled to find a way past Milan's rock-solid defense, defense match remained deadlocked at 0-0 after 90 minutes.

The game went into extra time, and it was then that Paolo made his mark. In the 110th minute, he picked up the ball on the edge of the Juventus penalty area and unleashed a powerful left-footed shot that sailed past Gianluigi Buffon and into the back of the net. It was a moment of pure magic, and it sealed Milan's victory and their sixth Champions League title.

Paolo's goal in that final was a fitting tribute to his incredible career. It demonstrated not only his defensive prowess but also his attacking instincts and his ability to score important goals when his team needed them the most. It was a moment that cemented his place in Milan's history, and it remains one of the most iconic moments in the history of the Champions League.

Overall, the Golden Age of Paolo Maldini was a time

of unmatched success for Milan and a testament to the incredible talent and leadership of one of football's all-time greats. It was a time that will be forever remembered by Milan fans and football fans everywhere, and Paolo's legacy as one of the greatest players ever to grace the game is secure.

5. THE ITALIAN STALLIONS: SUCCESS WITH THE NATIONAL TEAM

Paolo Maldini was not only a star for AC Milan, but also for the Italian national team. His international career spanned 14 years, during which he represented Italy in three World Cups and three European Championships, making him one of the most capped players in Italian football history.

Paolo's first major tournament with the national team was the 1988 European Championship in West Germany. Italy made it to the semi-finals before being knocked out by the Soviet Union. Paolo's performances in that tournament were impressive, and he was named in the team of the tournament.

Four years later, at Euro 1992 in Sweden, Italy was once again eliminated in the semi-finals, this time by the eventual champions Denmark. Paolo played every minute of Italy's five matches, and he was once again included in the team of the tournament.

It wasn't until the 1994 World Cup in the United States that Paolo and Italy finally tasted major international success. Italy made it to the final, where they faced off against Brazil in a match that would go down in history. Despite Paolo's best efforts, Italy was unable to secure the victory, and they were defeated 3-2 on penalties.

Paolo's performances at the 1994 World Cup were nothing short of outstanding. He was named to the team of the tournament, and he received the FIFA Fair Play Award for his conduct on and off the pitch.

Paolo's success with the national team continued into the late 1990s and early 2000s. Italy made it to the quarter-finals of the 1996 European Championship, the final of the 2000 European Championship (which they lost to France), and the round of 16 of the 2002 World Cup.

Throughout his international career, Paolo was a model of consistency and excellence. He was a leader both on and off the pitch, and he inspired his teammates with his unwavering dedication and commitment to the Italian cause. He was a true Italian stallion, a player who embodied the best qualities of Italian football and who will always be remembered as one of Italy's all-time greats.

Paolo Maldini's success with the Italian national team was a testament to his skill, determination, and leadership. He played an integral role in Italy's finest footballing moments and helped establish the national team as one of the best in the world.

Maldini's final international appearance came in the Euro 2002 quarter-final defeat to co-hosts South Korea, a controversial match that was marred by poor refereeing decisions. Despite the disappointing end to his international career, Maldini's legacy as one of the greatest players in Italian football history was secure.

Over the course of his international career, Maldini earned a total of 126 caps for Italy, scoring 7 goals. He also held the record for most appearances for Italy until he was surpassed by Gianluigi Buffon in 2013.

Maldini's contribution to Italian football was recognized in 2012 when he was inducted into the Italian Football Hall of Fame. He was also named in the FIFA 100, a list of the greatest living footballers selected by Pelé in 2004.

Even in retirement, Maldini remains a figurehead of Italian football. He has continued to be involved with AC Milan in a variety of roles, including sporting director and technical director. His knowledge, experience, and passion for the game have made him an invaluable asset to the club and to Italian football as a whole.

Paolo Maldini's success with both AC Milan and the Italian national team has cemented his place as one of the greatest footballers of all time. His legacy will continue to inspire future generations of players and fans alike, and his impact on the game will be felt for years to come.

Maldini's success on the pitch has also translated into success off the pitch. He is widely respected and admired for his professionalism, dedication, and sportsmanship, and has become a role model for aspiring footballers around the world.

In addition to his footballing achievements, Maldini is also known for his philanthropic work. He has been involved in several charitable causes, including raising money for cancer research and supporting underprivileged children in Italy and Africa.

Maldini's dedication to giving back to the community has earned him widespread respect and admiration. He is a true example of a sportsman who has used his success to make a positive impact on the world.

Overall, Paolo Maldini's legacy is one of greatness both on and off the pitch. He is a true legend of the game, whose skill, leadership, and passion for football have inspired generations of players and fans around the world.

Maldini's legacy also includes his impact on the sport of football itself. He was not just a great player, but a pioneer in the modern game, helping to redefine the role of the modern full-back.

Maldini's technical ability and intelligence on the pitch enabled him to play in multiple positions, but it was his work as a left-back that truly set him apart. His exceptional defending skills combined with his attacking prowess made him a potent force in both defedefense attacks.

Maldini's contribution to the sport was acknowledged in 2009 when h was awarded the UEFA President's Award, which recognizes standing achievement, professional excellence, and exemplary personal qualities.

In his acceptance speech, Maldini spoke of the importance of teamwork and unity, his success in football is not just about individual talent, but about the ability to work together as a team.

Maldini's legacy has had a lasting impact on the sport of football, inspiring future generations of players to strive for greatness both on and off the pitch. His dedication, hard work, and sportsmanship have earned him a place in the hearts of football fans around the world, and his legacy will continue to inspire and motivate players for generations to come.

In conclusion, Paolo Maldini is a true footballing

legend whose impact on the sport will be felt for years to come. His incredible achievements, both on and off the pitch, have made him a role model for aspiring footballers and a source of inspiration for fans all over the world. His legacy is one of greatness, sportsmanship, and dedication, and he will always be remembered as one of the greatest footballers of all time.

6. THE CAPTAIN: LEADERSHIP ON AND OFF THE FIELD

The legendary captain of AC Milan and the Italian national team, was known for his exemplary leadership both on and off the field. He was not just a captain, but a true leader who inspired and motivated his teammates to achieve greatness. Maldini was a true symbol of Milan, embodying the club's values and traditions, and he had could example, communicate effectively, and inspire his team to give their best.

On the field, Maldini's leadership was evident in his calm and composed demeanor. He led by example, always putting the team's needs above his own, and showing incredible dedication and passion for the game. He was a great communicator, constantly directing and encouraging his teammates, and had a rare ability to read the game and anticipate his opponent'.

Off the field, Maldini was just as influential. He was a role model for young players, always leading by example with his professionalism and dedication to his craft. He was a true ambassador for the sport, respected by players, coaches, and fans alike. Maldini's leadership extended beyond the pitch, as he was also known for his charitable work, using his influence to make a positive impact on the community.

Maldini's leadership was crucial in guiding Milan to their incredible success in the 1990s and 2000s, where they won countless trophies both domestically and internationally. His presence in the dressing room was a calming influence, and his ability to inspire his team to rise to the occasion was unmatched. Maldini's leadership also extended to the Italian national team, where he played a key role in their World Cup triumph in 2006.

Maldini's legacy as a leader and captain is undeniable. He was a true legend of the game, and his influence on the sport and the Milan community will be felt for generations to come. His leadership qualities have been studied and emulated by many, and he will always be remembered as one of the greatest captains of all time.

In conclusion, Paolo Maldini was not just a great

footballer, but a great leader. His ability to lead on and off the field was an inspiration to his teammates, and his legacy as a captain will be remembered for years to come. Maldini's leadership was a key factor in Milan's success, and his influence on the sport and community will never be forgotten.

Maldini's leadership was not just limited to his technical skills and ability to read the game. He possessed a great sense of sportsmanship and respect toward his opponents, earning him admiration from all over the world. He was a true gentleman of the sport, and his actions both on and off the pitch were a testament to his character.

One particular moment that showcases Maldini's leadership was during the 2005 Champions League final against Liverpool. Milan was as was at halftime, but a stunning comeback from Liverpool saw them level the game 3-3 by the end of the second half. Maldini, however, remained calm and composed, and rallied his team to regain their focus and composure. Despite the disappointment of losing the game, Maldini's leadership and character shone through, as he faced the media with grace and humility.

Maldini's leadership also extended to his role as a mentor to young players. He was known for taking new signings under his wing, and guiding them through the challenges of playing for a club as prestigious as Milan. His mentorship and guidance helped shape the careers of many young players, and contributed to the team's success in the long term.

Off the field, Maldini was a man of great integrity, and used his platform to make a positive impact on the community. He was involved in several charitable initiatives, and was a vocal advocate for environmental causes. His work off the field earned him widespread respect and admiration, and cemented his reputation as a leader both on and off the pitch.

In conclusion, Maldini's leadership was truly remarkable, and his impact on the sport of football and the community cannot be overstated. He was a true ambassador for the game, and his leadership qualities are something that young players can look up to and emulate. His legacy as a captain will live on, and he will always be remembered as one of the greatest leaders in the history of football.

7. THE ART OF DEFENDING: DEFENSIVE TECHNIQUES

For anyone who has ever played football, the importance of good defending cannot be overstated. When it comes to defending, few players have been as masterful as Paolo Maldini. Maldini, a former Italian professional footballer, was renowned for his technical ability, his tactical awareness, and his unwavering commitment to his team. In this chapter, we'll delve into the art of defending and explore some of Maldini's most effective defensive techniques.

One of the key skills that Maldini possessed was his anticipation. He had an uncanny ability to read the game and anticipate where the ball would be played. This allowed him to position himself in such a way that he could intercept the pass or make a crucial tackle. Maldini's anticipation was born out of his relentless studying of the game. He would watch hours of footage, analyzing the movements of players, and identifying patterns in their play. This allowed him to predict what his opponents were likely to do and adjust his positioning accordingly.

Another of Maldini's most effective defensive techniques was his use of his body. He was a master of positioning himself between the ball and his opponent, making it almost impossible for the player to get past him. He would use his body to shield the ball and use his arms to fend off any attempts to push him out of the way. Maldini's strength and physicality were a key part of his game, but he also knew how to use his body isubsubtly strategically

One of Maldini's most impressive defensive traits was his ability to tackle. He was a master of the slide tackle, which he would use to cleanly win the ball from his opponents without committing a foul. Maldini's tackling was a testament to his timing, his positioning, and his ability to read the game. He knew when to make a tackle and when to hold off, and he was always in the right place at the right time.

Finally, Maldini was an expert at one-on-one defending. He had a calm and composed demeanor that made it difficult for his opponents to rattle him. He would stand his ground, wait for the player to make a move, and then use his exceptional timing and agility to dispossess them. Maldini was a master of the art of defending, and his one-on-one defending was a key part of his game.

The art of defending is a crucial part of football, and few players have mastered it quite like Paolo Maldini. His anticipation, use of his body, tackling, and one-on-one defending were all key parts of his game, and they made him one of the best defenders of all time. For anyone looking to improve their defending, studying Maldini's techniques is a great place to start.

Maldini's skills on the pitch were not only down to natural ability. He also had an incredible work ethic and a dedication to his craft. He was known for his grueling training regimes, his attention to detail, and his willingness to constantly improve his game. Maldini was always looking for ways to push himself to the next level, both physically and mentally.

One of the key aspects of Maldini's defensive technique was his ability to stay focused for the full 90 minutes of a match. He was never caught out of position or caught off guard, as he was constantly aware of the game's dynamics. Maldini was able to maintain his concentration by keeping a clear mind, blocking out any distractions, and being fully present in then.

Maldini's leadership on the pitch was another crucial aspect of his game. He was a natural leader and commanded respect from his teammates. He would communicate with his fellow defenders, ensuring that everyone was in the right position and covering each other's backs. Maldini's leadership was especially important in big games, where the pressure was high and the stakes were even higher.

Despite his incredible talent, Maldini never became complacent or took his success for granted. He always remained humble, recognizing that there was always more to learn and improve upon. This attitude helped him to stay focused and motivated throughout his career, even in the face of adversity.

8. THE LASTING PARTNERSHIP: MALDINI AND NESTA'S DEFENSIVE DOMINANCE

Paolo Maldini was undoubtedly one of the greatest defenders of all time, but his success on the pitch was not solely down to his irilliance. Hbrillianceship with fellow Italian defender, Alessandro Nesta, was a crucial factor in Milan's defensive dominance in the early 2000s. In this chapter, we'll explore the unique partnership between Maldini and Nesta and how they were able to work together to create one of the most formidable defensive units in football history.

The partnership between Maldini and Nesta was built on mutual trust and respect. They had a deep understanding of each other's strengths and weaknesses, and they were able to complement each other perfectly. Maldini was a left-sided defender, while Nesta played on the right. Together, they formed a cohesive unit that was almost impenetrable.

One of the key aspects of their partnership was their communication. Maldini and Nesta would talk constantly throughout the game, making sure they were in the right positions and covering each other's backs. They would also provide each other with valuable feedback, helping each other to improve their game.

Their partnership was also built on their complementary skill sets. Maldini was renowned for his tactical awareness, his anticipation, and his ability to read the game. Nesta, on the other hand, was known for his physicality, his tackling ability, and his aerial prowess. Together, they formed a complete defensive unit that was able to handle any situation that came their way.

One of the most impressive aspects of their partnership was their ability to adapt to different opponents. They were able to adjust their playing style to counter the strengths of the opposition. Whether they were facing a pacey forward or a physical striker, Maldini and Nesta were able to adjust their defensive approach to neutralize their opponent's threat.

Maldini and Nesta's partnership was not only successful on the pitch but also off it. They had a deep personal relationship, and their friendship extended beyond the football field. This chemistry and understanding of each other were reflected in their defensive play, and it helped to make them one of the most successful defensive partnerships in football history.

The partnership between Paolo Maldini and Alessandro Nesta was a testament to the power of teamwork and communication. Their ability to complement each other's strengths and adjust their playing style to counter their opponents made them a formidable defensive unit. Their partnership was not only successful on the pitch but also off it, reflecting the importance of trust and respect in building successful partnerships.

Maldini and Nesta's partnership was a key factor in AC Milan's success during the early 2000s. Together, they helped Milan to win two UEFA Champions League titles and three Serie A titles. Their defensive dominance was crucial to Milan's success during this period, and they are still remembered today as one of the greatest defensive partnerships in football history.

After Maldini's retirement, Nesta continued to play for Milan for a further three seasons, but he was never able to replicate the same level of success without his defensive partner. The two players had formed an unbreakable bond on the pitch, and their partnership was sorely missed after Maldini's retirement.

Maldini and Nesta's partnership was not only successful because of their ialetalents but also the use of their shared dedication to their craft. They were both incredibly hardworking players who never took their success for granted. Their work ethic and dedication to the game were an inspiration to their teammates and fans alike.

In conclusion, the partnership between Paolo Maldini and Alessandro Nesta was a shining example of the power of teamwork and communication. They were able to complement each other's strengths and adjust their playing style to counter their opponents, making them one of the most successful defensive partnerships in football history. Their friendship and mutual respect off the pitch were reflected in their defensive play, and it helped to make them a truly legendary partnership.

9. THE END OF AN ERA: RETIREMENT

Paolo Maldini was a fixture at AC Milan for over 25 years. He was a true legend of the game and a leader both on and off the pitch. However, all good things must come to an end, and in 2009, Maldini announced his retirement from football. In this chapter, we'll take a look back at Maldini's incredible career and the impact that his retirement had on Milan and football as a whole.

Maldini's retirement marked the end of an era at Milan. He had been a cornerstone of the team for over two decades, and his leadership and defensive prowess had helped to make Milan one of the most successful clubs in football history. His retirement left a massive void in Milan's defense, and it was clear that the team would never be the same without him.

However, Maldini's legacy at Milan and in football

as a whole was secure. He had won seven Serie A titles, five European Cups, and countless other trophies during his career. He was also a key player for the Italian national team, helping them to win the 1982 World Cup and reach the final of the 1994 tournament. He was widely regarded as one of the greatest defenders of all time and a true ambassador for the game.

Maldini's retirement also had an impact on Milan's playing style. With Maldini no longer in the team, Milan's defense became less solid, and the team struggled to maintain the same level of dominance that they had enjoyed during Maldini's career. It was clear that Maldini's influence on the team had been immense, and his departure left a hole that was difficult to fill.

However, Maldini's retirement also provided an opportunity for new players to step up and make their mark on the team. The likes of Thiago Silva and Alessio Romagnoli were able to take on the mantle of Milan's defensive leaders, and they have gone on to achieve success in their own right.

Paolo Maldini's retirement marked the end of an incredible era at AC Milan. His impact on the team and football as a whole was immense, and his legacy as one of the greatest defenders of all time is secure. While Milan's defense may never be quite the same without him, his retirement also provided an opportunity for new players to step up and make their mark on the team. Maldini will always be remembered as a true legend of the game, and his influence on Milan and football as a whole will never be forgotten.

Maldini's retirement also had a wider impact on football as a whole. It marked the end of an era in which players like Maldini were able to spend their entire careers at one club. In the modern game, it is increasingly rare for players to remain loyal to one club for the entirety of their career, and Maldini's commitment to AC Milan was a rare and special thing.

Maldini's retirement also highlighted the importance of experienced players in football. In an era where young players are often given more opportunities than ever before, it is easy to forget the value of players like Maldini, who have years of experience and wisdom to draw on. Maldini's leadership and experience were invaluable to Milan during his career, and his retirement left a gap that was difficult to fill.

Finally, Maldini's retirement was a reminder of the fleeting nature of football careers. Despite his incredible success and longevity, Maldini was only able to play the game he loved for a finite amount of time. His retirement was a reminder to fans and players alike that football careers are short and that every moment on the pitch should be cherished.

In conclusion, Paolo Maldini's retirement marked the end of an incredible era at AC Milan and in football as a whole. His influence on the game was immense, and his legacy as one of the greatest defenders of all time is secure. While his retirement left a gap in Milan's defense that was difficult to fill, it also highlighted the importance of experienced players in football and the fleeting nature of football careers. Maldini will always be remembered as a true legend of the game, and his impact on football will be felt for generations to come.

10. THE MILAN DIRECTOR: ROLE IN CLUB MANAGEMENT

Following his retirement as a player, Maldini didn't stray far from AC Milan. He took on a new role at the club, serving as a director and working to help manage the team he had spent his entire career with.

As a director, Maldini brought the same passion and dedication to the club that he had as a player. He worked tirelessly to ensure that the team was performing at its best and that it was able to continue its long legacy of success. He was involved in all aspects of the club, from player recruitment to training and tactics, and his experience and knowledge of the game were invaluable in helping

Milan remain one of the top teams in Europe.

One of Maldini's key contributions as a director was his focus on youth development. Maldini recognized that, for Milan to continue its success, it was essential to build a strong youth academy and to develop young players who would be able to make a significant impact on the team in the future. Maldini worked hard to identify talented young players and to provide them with the support and resources they needed to succeed.

Maldini's commitment to Milan didn't go unnoticed by the club's fans. He remained a beloved figure at the San Siro, and his presence in the boardroom was a source of comfort to many supporters. His work as a director helped to cement his legacy at the club and ensured that his influence on Milan would continue long after his retirement as a player.

Maldini's role as a director at AC Milan demonstrated his continued commitment to the club and the sport of football. His focus on youth development and his dedication to ensuring that Milan remained one of the top teams in Europe were a testament to his enduring love of the game. Maldini's legacy at Milan will always be remembered, and his contributions to the club's success will continue to be felt for many years to come.

Maldini's experience as a player also played a crucial role in his work as a director. He was able to draw on his own experiences and insights to provide valuable guidance to the club's coaching staff and players. His knowledge of the game and his understanding of what it takes to succeed at the highest level was highly respected by everyone at the club.

One of Maldini's most significant accomplishments as a director was his work in rebuilding Milan's defense. In the years following his retirement as a player, Milan struggled to maintain the same level of defensive dominance that had been a hallmark of the club for so many years. Maldini recognize that needed to focus on rebuilding its defense if it was to return to its former glory.

Under Maldini's guidance, Milan's defense improved significantly. He oversaw the recruitment of several key players who helped to shore up the backline, and he worked closely with the team's coaching staff to develop new defensive strategies that would allow Milan to once again become one of the best defensive teams in Europe.

Maldini's work as a director was not without its challenges. He faced criticism from some quarters, who questioned his ability to transition from player to director. However, Maldini remained focused on his goals and his commitment to the club never wavered. His hard work and dedication paid off, and Milan once again became one of the top teams in Europe during his time as a director.

In conclusion, Maldini's role as a director at AC Milan was a testament to his love of the club and his passion for football. His experience and knowledge of the game were invaluable in helping Milan remain one of the top teams in Europe, and his work in rebuilding the team's defense was particularly noteworthy. Maldini's legacy at Milan will always be remembered, and his contributions to the club's success will continue to be felt for many years to come.

11. THE FAMILY MAN: PERSONAL LIFE

While Maldini was a legend on the football field, he was also a devoted family man off it. He was married to his wife, Adriana Fossa, for over 30 years, and the couple had two sons, Christian and Daniel.

Maldini's dedication to his family was evident throughout his career. Despite the demands of being a professional footballer, he always made time for his wife and children. He was known for his strong work ethic and his ability to balance his professional and personal commitments, and his family was always a top priority for him.

In many ways, Maldini's family life was a reflection of his approach to football. He understood the importance of teamwork, communication, and sacrifice, and he brought those same values to his family life. He worked hard to ensure that his family was happy and healthy, and he was always there for them, even when he was on the road with the team.

Maldini's family life was also notable for its stability. While many footballers struggle with the pressures of fame and the temptations that come with it, Maldini remained steadfast in his commitment to his family. He was always careful to maintain a low profile and avoid the spotlight, preferring to focus on his family and his football.

Maldini's family life was an important part of his identity as both a footballer and a person. His dedication to his wife and children, and his ability to balance his professional and personal commitments, were a testament to his strength of character and his unwavering commitment to those he loved. Maldini's legacy as a footballer will always be remembered, but his legacy as a devoted family man is equally important and will continue to inspire others for generations to come.

Throughout his life, Maldini maintained a strong connection with his family. Even after retiring from football and becoming a club director, he remained committed to spending time with his wife and children. In interviews, he often spoke about the importance of family and the joy that it brought him.

Maldini's sons, Christian and Daniel, also followed in his footsteps and became professional footballers.

Christian played for AC Milan and the Italian national team, while Daniel played for various teams in Italy and the United States. Maldini was a proud father and always supported his sons in their football careers.

In addition to his family life, Maldini was also known for his involvement in various charitable causes. He was a UNICEF Goodwill Ambassador and worked to raise awareness about the importance of education and child welfare. He also supported Fondazione Milan, a charitable foundation established by AC Milan to support disadvantaged children and young people.

Maldini's contributions to charity were a reflection of his values and his commitment to making a difference in the world. He understood the power of football to bring people together and to inspire positive change, and he worked hard to use his platform as a footballer to make a difference.

In conclusion, Maldini's personal life was a reflection of his values and his unwavering commitment to those he loved. His dedication to his family and his involvement in charitable causes were a testament to his character and his desire to make a positive impact on the world. Maldini's legacy as a footballer is well-known, but his legacy as a family man and a humanitarian is equally important and will continue to inspire people for many years to come.

12. THE FASHION ICON: INFLUENCE ON STYLE

Paolo Maldini was not only a footballing icon but also a fashion icon. The former AC Milan and Italy national team captain were renowned for his impeccable sense of style on and off the pitch. Maldini's fashion influence extended beyond his football career, and he became a global fashion icon in his own right.

Maldini's fashion style was characterized by a classic, timeless look that exuded sophistication and class. He was always impeccably dressed in tailored suits, stylish accessories, and sharp footwear. He was a master at combining different textures and patterns to create unique and stylish outfits.

Maldini was not afraid to take risks with his fashion choices and experimented with different styles throughout his career. He was one of the first footballers to wear a blazer to a pre-match press conference, and his bold fashion choices earned him praise from fashion critics around the world.

In addition to his style, Maldini also made an impact on the fashion industry through his work as a brand ambassador. He worked with a variety of luxury brands, including Dolce & Gabbana and Armani, and his endorsements helped to establish these brands as major players in the fashion industry.

Maldini's impact on the fashion world was not limited to his style and endorsements. He also made significant contributions to the development of football kits, working closely with manufacturers to ensure that the kits were both stylish and functional.

Maldini's influence on fashion extended far beyond the football pitch. His classic, timeless style and willingness to take risks made him a global fashion icon, and his work as a brand ambassador helped to establish luxury brands in the fashion industry. Maldini's legacy as a fashion icon will continue to inspire people for many years to come.

Despite retiring from football, Maldini's impact on the fashion industry continued to grow. In 2008, he launched his fashion line, "Sweet Years," which quickly became a popular brand in Italy and around the world. The brand's success was due in part to Maldini's reputation as a fashion icon, but also to his commitment to producing high-quality, stylish clothing at an affordable price point.

Maldini's influence on fashion extended beyond his brand, and he remained a sought-after model and brand ambassador. He was often seen attending fashion shows and events, rubbing shoulders with other fashion icons and designers.

Maldini's fashion influence was not limited to his style or brand. He was also a keen supporter of sustainable fashion and worked to promote eco-friendly fashion choices. He was a vocal advocate for ethical fashion practices and believed that the fashion industry had a responsibility to promote sustainability and ethical production methods.

In addition to his work in fashion, Maldini has also been active in other business ventures. He is the co-owner of Miami FC, a professional football club in the United States, and has been involved in a variety of other entrepreneurial projects.

Maldini's legacy as a footballing and fashion icon continues to inspire people around the world. His impeccable sense of style, commitment to sustainability, and entrepreneurial spirit have made him a role model for many. As he continues to make his mark in the business world, it is clear that Maldini's influence will be felt for many years to come.

13. THE PHILANTHROPIST : MALDINI'S CHARITABLE WORK

In addition to his work in football and fashion, Paolo Maldini has also made a significant impact through his philanthropic efforts. He has been involved in several charitable organizations throughout his career, using his platform and resources to make a positive impact in the world.

One of the causes that Maldini is most passionate about is environmental conservation. He has worked with several organizations dedicated to protecting natural habitats and wildlife and has been a vocal advocate for sustainable living practices. Maldini has also been involved in various projects to promote renewable energy, such as the installation of solar panels in schools and other public buildings.

Maldini is also committed to supporting children's charities. He has been involved with the United Nations Children's Fund (UNICEF) for many years and has used his position as a footballing and fashion icon to raise awareness and funds for the organization. Maldini has also been involved with various projects aimed at providing education and resources to underprivileged children, particularly in his home country of Italy.

In addition to his work with environmental and children's charities, Maldini has also been involved in projects related to health and disease prevention. He has been a vocal advocate for cancer research and has been involved with various organizations dedicated to finding cures and treatments for the disease.

Through his philanthropic work, Maldini has demonstrated a deep commitment to making a positive impact in the world. His dedication to environmental conservation, children's charities, and health initiatives has made a significant difference in the lives of many people around the world. As he continues to use his platform and resources to support these causes, it is clear that Maldini's legacy will be one of generosity, compassion, and service to others.

Maldini's philanthropic efforts have not gone unnoticed, and he has received numerous awards and recognitions for his work. In 2003, he was awarded the FIFA Fair Play Award for his commitment to environmental causes, and in 2005 he was honored by UNICEF for his contributions to the organization. Maldini has also been recognized by the Italian National Olympic Committee for his work in promoting healthy lifestyles and disease prevention.

Despite all of his accomplishments, Maldini remains humble and committed to using his influence for the greater good. He has spoken openly about the importance of giving back and has encouraged others to use their resources to make a positive impact in their communities.

In many ways, Maldini's philanthropic work is a reflection of his approach to life both on and off the pitch. Just as he was always committed to giving his all on the field and pushing himself to be the best player he could be, he has brought that same level of dedication and passion to his charitable endeavors. For Maldini, making a difference in the world is not just a hobby or a side project - it is an integral part of who he is as a person.

As Maldini continues to use his platform and resources to support environmental conservation, children's charities, and health initiatives, it is clear that his legacy will extend far beyond his achievements in football and fashion. He will be remembered not just as a great player and style icon, but as a true humanitarian who used his gifts to make the world a better place.

14. THE GLOBAL ICON: IMPACT ON FOOTBALL WORLDWIDE

Paolo Maldini's impact on football has extended far beyond his accomplishments on the pitch. As one of the greatest defenders in the history of the game, he has influenced generations of players with his skill, leadership, and dedication. But it is not just his playing career that has cemented his legacy as a global icon.

Maldini's influence can be seen in the way football is played and perceived worldwide. His commitment to fair play, sportsmanship, and respect for opponents has set an example for countless players and fans. His unwavering professionalism and commitment to excellence have inspired young players to pursue their dreams and strive for greatness.

But perhaps most significantly, Maldini's legacy is one of humility and class. Despite his many achievements, he has remained grounded and dedicated to the sport he loves. He has never been one to seek the spotlight or chase personal accolades, instead focusing on doing his job to the best of his ability and leading by example.

As a result, Maldini is widely respected and admired by players and fans around the world. His contributions to the game have been recognized with numerous awards and honors, including induction into the Italian Football Hall of Fame and the UEFA President's Award.

But for Maldini, the greatest reward has always been the love and support of the fans. He has spoken often of his gratitude for the passion and enthusiasm of football supporters and has made it clear that he sees his role as a steward of the game - someone who is responsible for upholding its traditions and values.

As Maldini continues to serve as a global ambassador for football, his impact will only continue to grow. He remains a role model for young players and a source of inspiration for fans around the world. And though he may have retired from playing, his legacy will endure for generations to come.

Maldini's influence has also extended to the world of coaching, where his expertise and knowledge have been highly sought after. After retiring from playing, Maldini took up a position as a technical director at AC Milan, where he was responsible for overseeing the club's transfer strategy and player development.

Under his guidance, the club has enjoyed a resurgence in recent years, with a renewed focus on youth development and a commitment to building a strong team culture. Maldini's understanding of the game and his ability to identify and develop talent has been crucial to this success, and his influence on the club's future is likely to be felt for years to come.

Beyond his work at AC Milan, Maldini has also been a vocal advocate for the development of football in emerging markets. He has worked closely with FIFA and other international organizations to promote the sport and to provide opportunities for young players to learn and grow.

In particular, Maldini has been a strong supporter of football in Asia, where he has traveled extensively to meet with young players, coaches, and fans. His presence and his commitment to the sport have helped to raise the profile of football in the region, and his insights and advice have been highly valued by players and coaches alike.

As Maldini's influence continues to be felt in the world of football, it is clear that his legacy is one of excellence, humility, and dedication. His commitment to the sport and his willingness to share his knowledge and experience with others have made him a true global icon, and his contributions to the game will continue to be felt for many years to come.

15. THE LEGACY CONTINUES: INFLUENCE ON FUTURE GENERATIONS

Maldini's legacy as a player and as a leader in the world of football has left a lasting impact on the sport, and his influence on future generations of players and coaches is sure to be felt for many years to come.

Through his dedication to excellence and his commitment to hard work and discipline, Maldini has set a standard for young players to follow. His technical abilities, tactical understanding, and leadership qualities have served as a model for many aspiring footballers, and his example has inspired countless others to strive for greatness.

But Maldini's influence extends beyond the field of play. His commitment to charitable work and his advocacy for social causes have set an example for young people around the world. His dedication to family, community, and the environment has helped to shape a new generation of leaders who are committed to making a positive impact on the world.

As Maldini continues to work as a coach, mentor, and ambassador for the sport, his influence on future generations of players and coaches is likely to continue to grow. His commitment to excellence, his dedication to teamwork, and his passion for the game are qualities that will continue to inspire young players and coaches for many years to come.

Ultimately, Maldini's legacy is one of excellence, leadership, and service. His commitment to the sport, his dedication to his team, and his tireless efforts to make a positive impact on the world have made him a true legend of the game, and his influence will continue to be felt for many generations to come.

In many ways, Maldini's legacy is still being written. As he continues to make his mark on the sport, his influence on future generations will only continue to grow. From his technical abilities and tactical understanding, to his leadership qualities and commitment to social causes, Maldini has left a lasting impression on the world of football.

But perhaps his greatest legacy will be the example he has set for future generations of players and coaches. By dedicating himself to excellence and hard work, by leading his team with passion and determination, and by always striving to make a positive impact on the world, Maldini has shown young people what it takes to be a true leader in the world of sports and beyond.

As Maldini himself once said, "You have to work hard to achieve your goals, but you have to enjoy it as well." This philosophy is at the heart of his legacy, and it is one that young players and coaches would do well to remember. By committing themselves to hard work, discipline, and a love for the game, they too can make their mark on the sport and inspire future generations to come.

In the end, Maldini's legacy is not just about what he achieved on the field, but about the example, he set for others to follow. Whether through his dedication to the sport, his commitment to social causes, or his tireless efforts to make a positive impact on the world, Maldini has shown us all that it takes to be a true leader, and his influence will continue to be felt for generations to come.

Printed in Great Britain
by Amazon